# THE HEAVENLY SEVEN
## STORIES OF THE MIGHTY ARCHANGELS

BY MELISSA DEAL FORTH

ILLUSTRATED BY ROBERT J. SCHWALB

ANDREWS AND McMEEL
A Universal Press Syndicate Company
Kansas City

Library of Congress Catalog Card Number 96-83992
ISBN Number 0-8362-0744-0

# CONTENTS

To Angela Page Brown,
Cindy T. Brown, and
Robert (Buzzy) Brown,
whose faith and support
made this book possible.

# INTRODUCTION
## HEAVEN

It began one magical day in heaven, a long, long time ago. God, with His Mighty face of Light and love, smiled with great joy as He sat upon his golden throne.

"Gabriel," He called out in a deep voice that rolled like thunder, "call forth My angels, so then they can share this happy day with Me." Gabriel blew her golden trumpet, a sweet and powerful sound, that reached every corner of heaven.

Immediately all God's angels stopped their work in heaven and rushed to His call. These angels were magnificent creatures of different sizes and shapes that could move at the speed of light. One by one the angels gathered about God's throne, their soft wings tucked beneath their flowing white gowns, their faces shinning in His presence.

God stood, arms outstretched, as great colors of the rainbow burst about Him. "Gather round, my children," He said, in a voice filled with joy. "Today I have created a most cherished place which I will put in *your* charge and under *your* protection."

"Behold," He said, and in the blink of an eye, the heavens separated. There, suspended in the sky, rotating around a blazing sun, were nine small planets.

"Look closer," He beckoned. And as if pulled under a giant magnifying glass, stood one lone planet. "This," He said in a voice full of pride, "shall be called Earth."

All the angels looked upon Earth in awe, for upon it were blue oceans filled with an assortment of life called, fish, whales, and smiling porpoises. There were majestic snow-capped mountains, golden wheat plains, green forests of trees, and gushing, flowing rivers, all abundant with new life-forms.

Some of the new life-forms were soft and furry, called mammals; some had tough, scaly skin, called reptiles. In the air flew beautifully colored winged creatures of different shapes and sizes, called birds, and the land flourished with thousands upon thousands of tiny creatures that flew and crawled, called insects. The earth was green and colorful from the many plants and flowers that covered and danced upon its meadows and hills.

The angels looked upon this day with great joy, sharing in God's happiness.

Then, in one swift movement of God's hand, lightning flashed and there upon Earth stood a creature unlike any of the others. "This," God said, with such love that tears of joy shone upon His face, "is My greatest creation of all, this is My beloved man, your brother."

Suddenly, a majestic roar rose from the depths of heaven, as a million streams of white light burst forth from God's finger into the heart of every man, woman, and child on Earth, and the angels saw upon this day, God's divine plan, that forever mankind would be a living part of God.

As God and his angels looked down upon this man and woman with joy, Lucifer, one of God's mightiest and most beloved angels, approached His throne.

Lucifer wore a beautiful tunic of woven white satin. His breastplate was made of gold, and about his waist was a sparkling jeweled belt, upon which hung a mighty sword of light. His knee-high boots were of fine red silk and his massive wings that spread from his shoulders were soft and white.

On bended knee and head bowed, Lucifer spoke to God. "My Lord, I have always been your faithful and obedient servant, but today I must protest this that you ask of me. I cannot serve these lowly creatures called man—their bodies are unlike ours, slow and heavy. Oh Mighty *Sir*, they can't even fly! It is you, God, I love, it is you alone I wish to serve. How can you ask this of an angel ranked as mighty as I?"

Slowly the bright smile of God began to fade. A thick silence engulfed the whole of heaven. "Lucifer," God said in disapproval, "look into My eyes." At this command, God's eyes blazed with a light so bright that Lucifer was forced to look away. "Now," God said in a thundering voice, "Look into the eyes of man, creatures you so boldly call lowly."

Lucifer turned his gaze upon earth and into the eyes of man. There he saw the same blazing light of God. "These creatures," proclaimed

God, "have been created in My Image, it is My Light that shines within their souls! Your pride and disobedience bring a great sorrow to heaven this happy day, Lucifer."

God said, now on His feet, His voice booming, "In not serving man you do not serve me. I have given all angels free will, the choice is yours, Lucifer, and yours alone."

Lucifer remained silent, and in his silence God knew that Lucifer had chosen not to serve man. "So be it," proclaimed God. "I see your choice is made, let it be done!"

God pointed His mighty finger to the door that led out from the throne room. "Go then!" God said, "You will never set eyes upon heaven again!"

Lucifer rose to his feet. Great pain was upon his face as he looked one final time into the face of his beloved Creator, then slowly he left. As Lucifer moved from the presence of God his clothes began to lose their glory and light. The beautiful jewels that adorned his belt fell to the floor, his breastplate of gold turned to tin, his glorious wings became spiky and gray, and his once mighty sword of light became a dull black sword of death. The light of God that once swirled about Lucifer was gone. Lucifer was now clothed in darkness and shadow.

God, watched sorrowfully as Lucifer left the throne room, then called out but one name . . . "Michael!"

Just the mention of his name brought a roar of cheers from the other angels. Great excitement filled the air as they stretched their necks to get a better look. Then, moving from God's left side, Michael stepped forward.

Michael was God's champion. He was tall with a muscular body. He was clothed simply in a short tunic of brilliant white linen with a breastplate of shining silver and a heavy woven silver belt at his waist, upon

which a mighty sword hung. Across his massive shoulders was a long cape of silver mail that hung to his feet covered with steel-blue knee-high boots. Golden curls covered his head whereupon a simple shining silver band sat. His aqua-blue eyes shone brightly from his handsome, strong face.

Michael did not look upon his Master's face but immediately fell to his knees with head bowed. His forty-foot wings of emerald closed about him in reverence to his beloved Creator.

All heavenly eyes were upon Michael. "My Lord," said Michael.

A smile of great pride crossed the face of God. It was with fondness that He spoke to the one before Him. "Arise, My loyal prince, let Me see thy face." At God's command, Michael stood tall before the Lord.

"This has been a day of great joy and sadness to Me," God said, sighing, "I know at this moment, Lucifer, in his jealous anger, gathers an army of darkness about him. It is for this reason I must call upon you, Michael, and six other of My most faithful angels, to take up the fight against this darkness, this evil that Lucifer will direct towards mankind and My new Earth."

God held out His hand, and in a burst of light a magical scroll appeared in it. "As I call your name," He said, "I ask that you stand with Me and Michael, to take up this fight for goodness and truth."

A great silence surrounded God's throne room. All the angels stood in excited anticipation, wondering which six angels would be chosen. God's mighty voice broke the silence as he called out the names.

"Gabriel!"

"Raphael!"

"Uriel!"

"Metatron!"

"Raziel!"

"Haniel!"

All the angels in heaven cheered loudly as each name was called.

One by one, these mighty angels proudly took their place in line next to Michael. God's voice was powerful as He spoke. "Today I call you seven together in the name of love. I will bestow upon each of you great gifts of power and strength. You will be the defenders, healers, teachers, and protectors of Earth." So, let it be known, as of this day forward, you are a new order of angels in heaven, today you become the divine Archangels, and forever, the Heavenly Seven!"

# CHAPTER ONE
## ARCHANGEL MICHAEL
## "CHIEF OF GOD'S ARCHANGELS"

As a new Monday morning broke, a very special week began in heaven. All the angels were excitedly rushing about, preparing for this glorious day. For this was the day Michael would be brought before God and given his assigned duties. This was the day Michael would receive his power!

All at once there was a great burst of trumpets and a heavenly sound was heard throughout heaven. God's throne room was beautifully decorated with gorgeous flowers, blooming fruit trees, and glorious, flowing banners of brilliant color.

Accompanied by several attending angels, God, in a superb robe of light, moved to His golden throne and was seated. There was a radiant smile upon His face. "Welcome, welcome," He said, as angel after angel gathered around him.

Then, with one mighty blast from the trumpets, Michael entered. Not knowing what this day would bring, he was humble in his presence.

Michael was escorted into God's throne room by two cherub angels with tiny wings. Here he was to meet his destiny; tears of joy filled his

blue eyes. He knelt before God, his great emerald wings now extended from his side at full length.

"Stand, My prince," God said.

"Today I bestow upon you great gifts of power that will allow you to fight against all evil in My name. There will be no power greater than the power of My Own. You will be known this day forward as 'Chief of God's Archangels'."

Then in one great burst of light, a glorious, golden shield appeared upon Michael's left arm. "This is My shield of truth, for which all that keep it will know My Grace," God announced. Suddenly, an exploding bolt of lightning cracked, and there within Michael's left hand appeared a golden lance. "This is My lance of protection, for which all that follow Me will find shelter." Then, in one final burst of exploding color, a mighty sword of blazing pure light appeared in Michael's right hand, so dazzling, so mighty, that all the angels of heaven fell down upon their knees. "This is My Sword of Justice, for all that practice it and love one another will know My promise of everlasting life!" God's voice boomed throughout the throne room.

All at once a great pillar of light began to swirl around Michael, a whirlwind of fire. Then, in one swift movement of God's hand, Michael stepped forward, out from the fiery tempest. Michael had been transformed! He was now clothed in a brilliant, luminous light. His simple short tunic was now made of a magic white, shimmering fabric and his breastplate had become a blazing glorious gold that burned the eyes if looked upon too long. The belt at his waist was now made of brilliant sparkling jewels, and his long cape had become a glorious deep scarlet, matching his knee-high boots. About Michael's head of curls was a shinning golden band and now upon his massive emerald wings appeared thousands of colorful eyes like a peacock's feathers!

In one swift movement Michael bowed to God, then turned to face the gathered angels. He held his blazing magic sword high into the air as blast after blast of lightning bolts shot from its tip, high into the heavens! The room exploded into cheers!

Michael turned back to God, and in a voice overwhelmed with love, he said, "Thank You, Father, thank You for this day, thank You for believing in me, I will not let You down."

"I know this Michael." God said. "Now, it is time we get to work!"

Michael made one final bow to his Lord, then, with sword held high above his head, he vanished in a burst of thunderous, exploding light, leaving behind a day of celebration in heaven.

Michael went at once to gather a mighty army of God's angels to fight Lucifer and his evil followers. There would be a ferocious battle in heaven, but Lucifer, no match for Michael and God's angels, would be cast out of heaven!

Since that time long ago, Archangel Michael has been watching over and helping all of God's people on earth. Today, with his magical sword of justice and powerful gifts from God, he fights all evil and darkness on earth.

Michael is known and serves all mankind, in all religions. In the Old Testament, it was Michael who stopped Abraham from sacrificing his son Isaac. Michael is believed to have been the author of Psalm 85, and, in ancient Jewish lore, it is Michael that is thought to have appeared to Moses upon Mount Sinai in the midst of the burning bush.

Joan of Arc, the young French peasant girl who led the French army to victory at the siege of Orleans in 1429, was said to have been counseled directly by the Archangel Michael.

Archangel Michael is a wondrous angel, ready to help and serve all God's children on earth, no matter what religion, creed or color. He has no boundaries and can be at our side in a moment's call. He stands ready to fight and protect all those that remember and teach . . . love.

# CHAPTER TWO
## ARCHANGEL GABRIEL
### "GOD'S MESSENGER"

As a brilliant Tuesday morning dawned in heaven, there was much excitement as angels sang glorious, happy songs, preparing for Gabriel's inauguration into the new order of Archangels. It was on this day that Gabriel, a shy and quiet angel, would stand before God and receive her assignment and gifts of power!

Michael, about to leave for his battle against Lucifer, stopped by Gabriel's preparation room to wish his dear friend a hearty congratulation. Gabriel understood that Michael could not stay, but the two embraced, knowing they would see each other again soon.

Suddenly the sound of many joyous trumpets began. All the happy and shinning angels took their place in God's throne room. God, in flowing robes of light, was escorted by His assistants to His golden throne. A buzz of excited voices and smiling faces filled the air.

Gabriel was led by her friend, the angel Uriel, to stand before God. Uriel's smile was exuberant as he looked upon her shinning face. Uriel bowed low before God, then took his place with the other angels.

Gabriel, on her knees, was dressed in her typical, modest white robe of light. About her waist was a single belt of silver, to which a silver horn was attached. Her beautiful, soft white wings were tightly held against her body. Her hair, a luxuriant fiery red, hung in a thick braid down her small back. A small, simple band of silver was about her head. Her green eyes were ablaze with excitement.

"Arise, Sweet Gabriel, " said God, with tremendous affection, "today it is with great pride and love I bestow upon you, My gentle servant, My Voice. You will be known as 'My Messenger'!"

Gabriel faced God with shinning eyes. God pointed His majestic finger in Gabriel's direction, as an exploding tempest of swirling color shot from its tip, surrounding Gabriel. In a split second her modest gown had become a brilliant white tunic, bordered in shining gold. Hanging from her small, slender shoulders was a glorious golden cloak of mail that hung to her feet. Suddenly . . . a thunderbolt exploded against Gabriel's chest and in a flashing blast of light, her once tiny silver horn blazed! It was now a magnificent golden instrument of light, hanging upon a glorious belt of dazzling red, red rubies.

"This horn, Gabriel," the Lord explained, "shall announce to all of My creation, the Word of God."

Gabriel's magnificent wings now sparkle with millions of tiny white lights that twinkle like stars. Her knee-high boots matched the sparkling gold that bordered her tunic and cloak. The simple silver band upon her head had become one of gold, set with sparkling red rubies. Woven into her mane of fire were delicate golden threads. A powerful white light glowed all about her.

"Thank You, Lord, for Thy trust." Gabriel said in her soft musical voice. " It is with great honor I accept my mission in Your name. It is with great honor that I serve my man and woman and Earth."

The entire room of angels jumped to their feet, breaking into one tremendous roar of heavenly song!

God, smiled broadly, then held up His hand, quieting the room.

"Gabriel, My Voice," the Lord continued, "today I send you out from heaven. Your mighty horn shall announce to all My children, to all life on Earth, My presence, My love, My Word. These gifts of power I have given you will assist you in your task, for there is no darkness or evil that can penetrate the light and love of God. Go now and tell them, I *am* with them!"

Immediately, at God's command, Gabriel took flight, her mighty wings spread wide as she rose, suspended high above the throne room. Gabriel placed the golden horn to her lips and in one mighty blast . . . she disappeared in a spark of light toward Earth.

As Gabriel flew to Earth, she could hear the heavenly voices of all her angel friends singing. She knew they would be singing into the night.

From that day forward and throughout history, Gabriel has appeared to Earth's children as God's Messenger.

It was Gabriel who appeared to the biblical prophet Daniel in a burst of white light, telling him of the coming Messiah, a message she repeats a millennium later (one thousand years) to the Virgin Mary of the coming birth of Jesus.

In ancient Muhammadan lore, it is the Archangel Gabriel (Jibril in Islamic) that dictated to Muhammad the entire Koran, the sacred book of the Muslims.

Archangel Gabriel is also thought to have directed Joseph of Arimathea to bury the Holy Grail, the cup used by Jesus at the Last Supper, in Glastonbury, England. This is the site where the first Christian church would be built in Great Britain.

Then again, in the not so distant future, the Holy Grail was thought to have been lost. It's Gabriel that descends from heaven to Castle Corbenic, delivering the Holy Grail to the famed knight of Arthurian legend, Sir Galahad.

Later, Galahad, with two other grail knights—Perceval and Bors—are said to have been divinely guided by ship to the distant city of Sarras. There Gabriel, accompanied by two other angels, appear to the three knights, where, upon rising into heaven with the Holy Grail, it is never seen again.

Archangel Gabriel is, like all of God's angels, a loving, caring angel, always ready to help the people of Earth. It is said we can all hear her golden horn and its messages of love today . . . all we have to do is listen to our hearts.

## CHAPTER THREE
## ARCHANGEL RAPHAEL
## "THE HEALER"

As the week of celebration continued in heaven, everyone was jubilant. Thousands of angels flew here and there as they prepared for a glorious Wednesday and the inauguration of the angel Raphael.

Unlike the shy, quiet Gabriel, Raphael was known throughout heaven as a personable and outgoing angel with a quick smile. All of God's angels busied themselves in excited preparation as they wondered what wondrous gifts would be bestowed upon their good-natured friend.

One by one the shining angels gathered in God's throne room. The great banners of color waved, as choirs of angels sang heavenly songs. Suddenly, hundreds of trumpets in unison announced the arrival of God.

God, in all His majesty, entered His golden throne room escorted by beautiful angel attendants. His face blazed bright with joy, His flowing robes of brilliant light flashed about Him.

Then, one single trumpet sounded as Raphael was escorted before God. He was most unlike any of God's angels in his dress. Raphael carried only a long pilgrim's staff and dressed in a simple robe of white with only a small cord about his waist.

His wings were tucked under his robe unseen. His hair was a shining auburn that fell in long curls about his shoulders, a great smile shone upon his face.

"Raphael," God said, with a twinkle in His eye, aware of Raphael's playful disposition, "step forward."

Raphael stepped forward and dropped to his knees before the Lord, his eyes brimming with tears of joy and excitement.

God rose to His feet and thousands of mighty bursts of colored lights exploded about Him. "Rise, My loyal servant," God said, in a voice that was strong and full of love. "Today I bestow upon you great gifts of power!"

Raphael stood, as a great lightning bolt shot from God's mighty finger and blasted upon him. Immediately Raphael was surrounded by the fiery tempest of God. Thousands of brilliant lights shot high into the heavens, bursting into marvelous colors of the rainbow. The powerful winds of God swirled and danced about Raphael.

At God's command Raphael stepped out of the swirling tempest. He was no longer clothed in a simple robe, but had become a radiant being of light! His new robe was now a blazing garment of gold, his once small belt now sparkled with thousands of shining emeralds, and upon his auburn head of curls sat a matching emerald crown! His unseen wings had become a brilliant golden yellow that stretched proudly from his shoulders!

Raphael was amazed, he could not help but marvel at his new heavenly clothes. "My Lord," Raphael called out in delight, "I am beautiful!" God could not help but chuckle at Raphael's innocent statement. "Why yes, Raphael, you are beautiful," God said, "but we are not finished yet!"

Just at that moment, in a flash of exploding light, a staff of pure gold, as bright as the sun, appeared in Raphael's hand.

"This magic staff, Raphael," the Lord explained, "will accompany you on your journey to Earth, for as of this day you will be known as 'My Healer.' Your task is to administer to the sickness and pains that will afflict the people and animals of earth, for though they are of My spirit inside, which is everlasting, their outer body is of flesh and bone and will need loving care.

"I have given you great knowledge of healing in My name, Raphael," continued God, "of which you will share and teach the children of Earth. For they will know through your compassion and love My compassion and love!"

In one quick move Raphael, his face beaming, bowed to the Lord. The room exploded in cheers from the heavenly host of angels, knowing what a great honor the Lord had given this happy little angel.

Raphael, holding his golden staff high towards the heavens, took flight in a burst of light, pausing only a moment to look again upon the shining face of God. Then, with his beautiful yellow wings spread wide, he flew out from the blue heavens toward Earth.

Since that time in heaven long ago, Archangel Raphael has been known as God's Angel of Healing.

Jewish legend believes that it was Raphael that handed Noah a "medical book" after the great flood to help him treat his family and the many animals that were in Noah's care.

Raphael is said to carry a pilgrim's staff and likes to travel in disguise, hiding his mighty wings so well that many times we come face to face with Raphael, not realizing we are talking to an angel! He is said to have a jesting nature with a quick wit, teaching us the power of laughter and a smile.

Many believe that Raphael is also the angel of joy, love, prayer, and hope. However, in the ancient Greek tongue, from which much of the English language comes, Raphael means . . . healing angel.

Archangel Raphael comes to comfort us whenever we are sick. We can be in the hospital, at home, or just feeling sad. He has no boundaries and knows at once when he is needed. He cares not what color our skin is, where we live, how smart we are, or of what religious faith we may be. He loves us one and all, reminding us always of God's love and that we are never alone.

## CHAPTER FOUR
### ARCHANGEL URIEL
### "THE LIGHT OF GOD"

As a new dawn broke on this glorious Thursday morning, singing, angelic voices, accompanied by beautiful music could be heard throughout all the great white marble halls in heaven.

Angels were everywhere, busily arranging newly bloomed flowers, hanging colorful banners on the majestic white columns, and rehearsing with their harps in joyous song, for today would be the day that angel Uriel would receive his great gifts and power!

As last-minute preparations were made, a single trumpet sounded, sending angels scurrying to their places. Moments later, a thousand trumpets broke into song as God and his attending angels entered the throne room.

"Sit, sit, My children," God said, as He sat upon His golden throne. "We have another wonderfully exciting day before us."

God nodded His head to the trumpeters and at once a magical note announced the angel Uriel, who upon entering the throne room, went down on bended knee before the Lord.

Uriel, was a small, quick angel, dressed simply in a short, violet tunic

with a golden belt. His hair was the color of wheat, cut short about his head. His wings were large, made of soft white feathers tucked closely to his body. He had a single band of gold about his head and short golden boots upon his feet.

"Stand, dear Uriel," God said lovingly.

Uriel moved to his feet. His eyes, like his tunic, were a sparkling, shinning violet.

Then, a single blast from God's mighty finger engulfed Uriel in a heavenly fiery tempest. The wind swirled, lightning flashed, thunder rolled through the great halls. Uriel was completely covered by this whirling cloud of fire and wind.

Then silence . . . as slowly, slowly, the twirling winds subsided and there, standing alone, surrounded in a magnificent light, was Uriel! In one hand he held Earth with its orbiting moon, in the other he held the Sun, and all about him were twinkling stars. His tunic had become a brilliant deep purple, like a clear night's sky, his belt was a blazing gold with a glowing comet buckle, and upon his head was a golden cap made of the planets, Mercury, Venus, Mars, Jupiter, Saturn, Uranus, Neptune, and Pluto! His wings, a brilliant white, extended fully from his shoulders.

"Loyal Uriel," God's voice thundered, "as of today, you will always be known as, My 'Angel of Light'!" Suddenly, the heavens opened wide and a great chariot of fire, drawn by two flashing white horses with huge wings, landed at Uriel's side. "Go!" said God, "tell the children of Earth that in the light they will find Me always!"

Uriel mounted the fiery chariot, taking the golden reins in his hand. A fiery flame billowed from the nostrils of the mighty horses. Instantly they took flight, the horses' giant wings spread wide as they soared high into the clouds towards the stars! Explosion after explosion of dazzling colorful fireworks burst everywhere as Uriel streaked across the heavens like a blazing white comet toward Earth!

Since that time long ago in heaven, Archangel Uriel has been watching over the Sun, moon, planets, and stars, keeping them on course and in their rotational orbits.

Uriel is also thought to be the angel sent by God, to warn Noah of the coming flood, telling Noah that he should prepare the ark to "save" his family and Earth's animals from the flood.

Archangel Uriel is said to be one of the angels that stands at our side, whispering in our ear, giving us clarity, reminding us of the importance of always telling the truth. Believed to be the angel with the sharpest eyes, he sees and knows when we are about to make a mistake, then moves quickly to offer us guidance in the right direction.

Uriel can also be a very tough angel, rushing in to deal swift punishment to bad people or dark forces that try to lead God's children from doing the right thing, for he loves God's children very, very much and is constantly watching over them.

# CHAPTER FIVE
## ARCHANGEL METATRON
### "GOD'S CHANCELLOR ANGEL"

The next glorious morning in heaven found sleepy angels rising early from their beds in preparation of a most unusual celebration day. This Friday, the tallest and biggest angel, Metatron, would stand before God and receive his gifts of power! He is said to be so tall that he can stand on Earth while his head is in heaven! Much preparation had to be done to accommodate such a big, big, angel.

All angels have the power to make things bigger or smaller. They simply whisper sweetly to this flower or gently touch that flower and happily the flowers burst up, up, up. In fact, this day the roof in the great throne room had vanished altogether so the giant flowers could poke their lovely heads up into the clouds!

Suddenly, the trumpets sounded and all the angels took a seat high upon fluffy, floating white clouds so they could see the mighty Metatron better.

Then in a magical flash of bright light, God suddenly appeared seated upon his golden throne! He and His throne had now become much, much bigger, taller than even Metatron!

Again the trumpets blew, and the giant Metatron entered the throne room and stood before God. He was so big that with each step he took the sound of thunder rolled and vibrated throughout the great halls. His wings were so massive that angels sitting high upon the clouds, looking down, could not see them from top to bottom.

"My Lord," Metatron said, as he kneeled before his creator.

"Stand and move closer, old friend," God said. "It is with overflowing joy that we meet this day, for I have great gifts of power and responsibility to bestow upon you."

Metatron was known as a fierce but gentle warrior, one of the first angels created by God in the early days of heaven. They loved and knew each other well.

Metatron stood, pulling his massive wings under control, aware of their mighty size.

Just as Metatron reached his feet he was hit with God's blazing tempest of fire, nearly knocking him over. Instantly he was covered with the fiery winds, surrounded in a column of color and light. As the winds of this mighty fire swirled and whirled about him he stood tall, unafraid.

God called out to him. "Metatron, Metatron . . . come forward." Lightning and thunder flashed and rolled about them.

All became quiet in the throne room as there before God stood an angel so bright, so magnificent, that the angels in heaven broke out in glorious songs of cheer. Metatron towered above the throne room, now majestically dressed in a robe and cape made entirely of fire! Beautiful flames of blue, purple, and orange burst about him in all directions, some shooting high into the sky. His tremendous wings were outstretched and glowed a deep red.

Metatron's eyes blazed a brilliant ice-blue and his face shone with a heavenly light!

Suddenly, from out of nowhere appeared a glowing, fiery scroll in Metatron's hand. "You, Metatron, will be known as 'My Chancellor of Heaven'!" said God. "Within your hand you hold the mighty book of life, in which the name of each and every man, woman, and child upon Earth is held. It is within this heavenly book that you will record every deed of kindness, forgiveness, and unconditional love that my beloved children perform on Earth. You will also record their acts of meanness and hatred. I will know all there is to know about ever human on Earth. It is with this knowledge we will guide them to greatness and glory!

"You, Metatron," God continued, "will be the link between the human and the divine!"

Archangel Metatron is said to be a loving and caring angel of people of all religions and color. He is thought to have been the author of Psalm 37:25 and, according to ancient Jewish lore, it was Metatron that led the children of Israel through the wilderness, which caused him to sometimes be referred as the "liberating angel." It is also as the liberating angel that, upon God's command, he leads our souls in complete love and without fear to heaven, where we will live forever with our families, God, and His angels.

Some believe Metatron himself teaches and guides all the little children that come to heaven from Earth, showing them the wonders of heaven where all dreams come true. Metatron is there for all who call upon him . . . all you have to do is ask.

# CHAPTER SIX
## ARCHANGEL RAZIEL
### "SECRET OF GOD"

Angels are everywhere, racing about as they prepare for a full, new day of festivities. It is upon this day that both Angel Raziel and Angel Haniel will be brought, one at a time, before God to receive their great gifts and powers!

This is in honor of God's law that Sunday be the day of rest. So you see, this wondrous Saturday will be extra busy and extra special.

All of heaven's angels were in a rush as they dashed and flew on white wings from room to room, decorating the throne room with thousands of singing colorful flowers and great banners of color that streamed and flowed from one majestic column to another.

All at once a thousand thunderous trumpets sounded. Quickly, all the angels quieted down as God in his blazing, flashing robes of white entered the room. He smiled and nodded to all the angels. "Welcome, welcome, my shining ones," He said tenderly, meeting their glowing faces with His loving smile.

Once seated, God signaled to a single trumpeter and, instantly, a beautiful sound flowed out from his horn. So beautiful was the melody

that small, beautiful flowers popped, with smiling faces, out from the mouth of the horn! The amused angel trumpeter smiled back at the little flower faces before him.

Upon this sweet sound, Raziel entered the golden throne room and fell to his knees, hands clasped together in his lap.

Angel Raziel was known as a studious angel. When his duties were finished for the day he could always be found in heaven's great library, reading and studying the laws of God. He was fascinated with all creation, but had lately been thrilled with God's new Earth and its lovely new people and animals that lived there.

Raziel was also quick—able to fly at great speeds. He wore a blazing white tunic and a braided belt made of shining woven threads of silver and gold. Upon his feet were golden knee-high boots with tiny wings at their heels. Some say this was why he could fly so fast!

"My Great Lord," Raziel said.

"Stand, Raziel, my studious little one!" the Lord commanded lovingly.

All of a sudden there was a mighty sound of wind rushing through the halls. The angels looked all around the room as the sound became a roar. Louder and louder it came, building like rolling thunder about them, then . . . it appeared. The wind—it was alive! It whipped and flashed through the throne room, surrounding Raziel, engulfing him in a mighty funnel of whirling white clouds like a tornado!

The colorful banners were ripped from their columns, the flowers closed their petals tightly about their faces against the wind. Angels were blown from their seats and sent high into flight, high above the throne room! Great colors flashed and exploded in the air.

Just as suddenly . . . it stopped. Angels were set back softly and small flower faces peered out from their petals to gaze upon the magic about them.

Raziel stood tall with his arms at his side. His eyes were now two shin-

ing torches of light. No longer was his tunic a simple white but had become a dazzling, deep royal blue, bordered in a blazing gold trim of tiny golden stars. A rich, royal blue velvet cape reached to his feet and his belt was wide and shone with brilliant sparkling sapphires from which a magic jeweled sword hung. His knee-high boots were a matching royal-blue satin as the tiny golden wings at his heels glowed and flapped. The mighty wings upon his shoulders were now feathers made of pure soft gold and, upon his head of black curls, was a thin golden band made of millions of tiny flashing blue sapphires!

God's loving, thunderous voice called out. "Raziel, step forward!"

Raziel stepped forward at God's command. Then, suddenly, in one fiery blast a great book appeared in his hand. "This, Raziel, is My book of knowledge. With it you will counsel and teach mankind to become scientists, mathematicians, teachers, writers, artists, and doctors. It is through this book that I bestow upon you many magical gifts.

"From this day forward," God said lovingly, "you will be known as the 'Secret of God' and from this book of knowledge you will teach My children of Earth My many secrets. It will be up to you to guide them toward the right path, revealing to them the answers to their questions through their parents, religious leaders, books, schools, and dreams. Tell them if they will choose love and forgiveness then all of the mysteries of the universe and all of the knowledge of life, I will hand unto them freely!"

Raziel was radiant! For all the gifts he could have wished God to have given him, none could be as grand as these. "Thank you, Lord," Raziel said, his voice full of emotion.

At once Raziel was lifted into flight by a great surge of wind, his golden wings spread wide. As he smiled down to the Lord with great appreciation, he then, in one great blast of lightning, turned and soared toward Earth, the great book in his hand and a smile of joy upon his face!

Archangel Raziel is called "the Secret of God," meaning he is the angel that oversees secret places and supreme mysteries. In ancient Jewish lore, he is believed to be the angel of divine wisdom.

It is Raziel who was thought to have delivered this book of knowledge to Noah, which explained in detail to Noah how he was to build his famous and wondrous ark. It is said that each day Archangel Raziel stands high upon the mountains of Earth, his wings spread wide, reading from this mighty book from God, proclaiming the secrets of knowledge to all mankind. We are all born knowing right from wrong, so if we close our eyes and listen to our hearts, we can hear Raziel teaching us from the mountains!

Another of Raziel's jobs, is to teach mankind how wonderful our planet is. It is Raziel that reminds us to take care of our Earth, the animals and plants that live upon it, that they too are created and loved by God, that they too have a right to be here and respected. We must remember that when God gave us power over the animals and plants, He did not mean we were to kill and mistreat them, but to help and protect them, as God's angels help and protect us.

You too can be an angel upon our Earth and help the Archangels; all you have to do is love and forgive one another and always show kindness.

It is said that the angels in heaven cry heavy tears when we are unkind to one another, Earth, and the beautiful animals we share it with.

# CHAPTER SEVEN
## ARCHANGEL HANIEL
### "GLORY OF GOD"

All the angels cheered from the clouds as they watched Raziel fly past galaxy after star-filled galaxy toward Earth.

No sooner had Raziel flown out of sight than a blast of trumpets announced the arrival of the mighty angel known as Haniel.

Haniel was a wondrous angel, dressed in a short, tan tunic. A single, striped belt of woven copper hung about his waist on which a single scabbard and sword hung. His hair, a shining brown, fell long, down his back, in a ponytail. His eyes blazed a brilliant blue. His knee-high boots were of woven tan satin that glistened with golden light.

God smiled and sat upon His golden throne when Haniel entered His holy room. Haniel dropped to his knees before the Lord. "Father," he said, head bowed.

"Stand, My son Haniel," the Lord said. "Today I honor your undying loyalty, today I call you forth to meet your destiny!"

Haniel stood as the heavens opened above him and God's tempest of fire came down upon him. Again and again could be heard the thunder of this mighty, fiery wind, blasting, swirling around him. Lightning

flashed as brilliant bursts of color exploded throughout the throne room!

Slowly . . . slowly, the winds began to subside and there, out of the fiery tempest, stepped Haniel! His short tunic was a brilliant fabric of gold! Clasped tightly upon his mighty chest was a shinning golden breastplate and around his waist a jeweled scabbard and golden sword hung! Upon his left shoulder appeared a golden bow with twenty-three golden arrows nestled within a mail golden pouch! His knee-high boots were made of a thin golden mail that clung tightly to his muscular calves and a singular golden band sat upon his head.

Haniel's strong wings stood back proudly from his shoulders, now a soft golden yellow, that not only moved him faster than light, but also at the speed of thought! All we have to do is "think" of an angel and Haniel is there beside us!

"You, Haniel, will be the 'Glory of God'," God proclaimed. "Your gifts are your bow and arrows of compassion and mercy. Your arrows will shoot straight into the hearts of all of My people, able to destroy any evil that may surround them or lead them down the wrong path. Your arrows will have the power to remind them that no matter what their mistakes may be, they can change, that I have sent angels to Earth to help them, and they can be anything they want to be!"

Haniel bowed low to God. "This, Lord, is the greatest of gifts You have given to me. I will go to Earth and tell Your children of these wonders that surround them. I will tell them that there is not a man, woman, child, or bird that flies, not a creature of the sea, not an animal that roams Earth, or a blade of sweet grass, or the smallest of insects that You did not create, that You do not love."

Haniel rose to his feet and in one mighty jump leaped high into the air, his outspread wings carrying him up, up, up. He circled the throne room, then, taking on great speed, he disappeared in a thunderous blast of glorious colors toward Earth!

Instantly, brilliant fireworks burst high into the heavens as the last of "the Heavenly Seven" made his way to help and protect the children of Earth.

Haniel is a wondrous angel known throughout heaven for his loyalty, courage, and fairness. He rules the month of December and, like all of the angels, lives each day following the golden rule: "do unto others as we wish others to do unto us."

Some believe that the mythical stories of the bow-and-arrow-clad cherub known as Cupid might really be Haniel in disguise! And every February 14, when we celebrate Valentine's Day, Haniel magically changes into a cuddly, roly-poly little angel, who flies all over the world on tiny wings, shooting Earth's people with his invisible arrows made of light. It is as "Cupid" that Haniel reminds us to always love one another, that we are all part of God's family and all loved equally by Him.

Haniel is also known to have the most beautiful singing voice in heaven. It is said that on quiet nights when the crickets and whippoorwills sing, it is because they can hear Haniel's heavenly voice and are singing along with him!

We, too, can hear Haniel's wondrous voice if we but listen in the night. For he is always there, teaching us through a sweet lullaby that there is nothing to be afraid of in the dark. For God and his angels are with us night and day; they *never* leave us.

So each night before you go to bed, remember, there is a beautiful angel who sits by your bed while you sleep, keeping watch over you *all night long*.

# EPILOGUE
## THE GIFT

Angels move invisibly in and out of our lives daily, able to take on any shape, form, or color of skin they choose. They have such magnificent powers that they can appear as our grandparents, a fireman, or even as a loving pet, guiding us and leading us away from danger. They can come to us in our dreams and they always, always, speed our prayers to God upon their mighty wings of light.

God gave all the children of Earth "free will," which means we have the right to choose between good and bad. God and His angels hope that you will always choose to tell the truth, to do good, and always show kindness and love to the people and animals that share our wonderful planet Earth. God knows that sometimes this is hard to do, but you can do it, keep trying!

God wants you to know you are never alone, no matter who you are or where you live, there is always an angel at your side to help you, to be your best friend. Even if you can't always see them, they are there, protecting and watching over you and your family!

Angels are God's special gift to us, sent down from heaven, wonderful friends who are always there to talk to, to hold you, to love you. Never, ever forget that God loves us more than anything and always hears our prayers.

So remember, believe in miracles, for *you* are a miracle, so important and so special are you to God that He has sent his powerful, Mighty Angels to always be with you!

So our stories begin! Come along with the
Mighty Archangels, Michael, Gabriel, Raphael,
Uriel, Metatron, Raziel, and Haniel,
as they use their glorious gifts and powers
from God to fight the evil deeds of Lucifer
through time and history on Earth!
Coming Soon . . .
*The Adventures of
The Heavenly Seven,
Book II*